AF430492

PAPA AND HIS RV

# Dedication

This book is dedicated to my parents, Martha and the late James Brown. Thank you for supporting and loving me. There wasn't a parent book on this earth to prepare me for my eccentricity. I appreciate you coming to my football games in college in our beautiful white RV. The RV that you bought for our family was the vessel to spend more time, build more memories, improve quality of life, and an inspiration of universal freedom. Riding around during Christmas time in the RV will be a memory I'll never forget. For us, owning a RV was THE AMERICAN DREAM. It's life altering when you can put that RV on the road and go wherever your heart desires. Love Dana

"Wake up, Crystal, Dennis, and Tony! Brush your teeth and wash your faces! We are jumping in the RV to visit a few special places. Pack your bags, grab our map, and don't forget your baseball caps. Get ready; we will travel the states, hurry up; there's no time to waste!" Papa shouts. Our Papa loves his RV, and he doesn't care where we go. "Let's hop in the RV it's time to hit the road! "First stop, Chicago," Papa says.

It took our Papa and us 5 hours to get here, but we finally made it. Our Papa loves the Cubs baseball team, so we stopped to watch a game. Papa screams every time there is a homerun! We enjoyed going to the Sears Tower, which is the second tallest skyscraper in the U.S. It has 108 floors, but don't worry, we took the elevator. Our Papa and us ate Chicago style pizza at Rocko's, and it was simply delicious. Last, Papa took us to his old neighborhood on 96th and Luella Street. Papa had tears in his eyes because it brought back so many memories. "Hop in the RV! Second stop, St. Louis!" Papa says.

It took our Papa and us 4 hours to get here, but we finally made it. Papa took us to the Gateway Arch. It's made from stainless steel and was built in 1965. We can see the entire city when we look out of its windows. Papa is crazy about the Botanical Garden. It is an Indoor and outdoor rainforest. It has 79 acres of historical gardens. Our Papa took us to eat famous St. Louis Style ribs. They were sweet, tender and smokey! "Hop in the RV! Third stop, Keystone, South Dakota!" Papa says.

It took our Papa and us 14 hours to get here, but we finally made it. "Wow, what are those faces!" Dennis yells. "It's Mount Rushmore," Crystal says. "It's a National Memorial on Black Elk Peak," Tony exclaims. "Yep, President Roosevelt, Lincoln, Jefferson, and Washington are carved from granite," momma announces. "What a site to see!" Papa shouts. "Hop in the RV! Fourth stop, Seattle," Papa says.

It took our Papa and us 18 hours to get here, but we finally made it. Our Papa took us to the Space Needle. "The Space Needle stands 605 feet tall. It takes 43 seconds to travel to the top inside of the elevator," Papa said. Crystal, Dennis and Tony screamed to the top of their lungs! "Hop in the RV! Fifth stop, Los Angeles," Papa says.

It took our Papa and us 17 hours to get here, but we finally made it. "Oh Yeah, Oh Yeah, OHHHH YEAH! Hollywood city! "Good Gracious Alive! Hollywood city!" Papa sings. We know that we have arrived because our Papa loves movies. This is the place where movies are made. "Hop in the RV! Sixth stop, San Francisco," Papa says.

HOLLYWOOD

It took our Papa and us 5 hours to get here, but we finally made it. "We have to cross the Golden Gate Bridge," Papa says. "It's so red and pretty!" Crystal shouts. "We're scared," Dennis and Tony whispered. "Don't be scared, will you look at all of that beautiful water. We will get across safely" momma exclaimed. "Hop in the RV! Seventh stop, Las Vegas," Papa says.

It took our Papa and us 9 hours to get here, but we finally made it. "The city that never sleeps! Let's go to the circus," Crystal said. There was a potent smell of cotton candy and popcorn that filled the air. Clowns were everywhere tying balloons into animals. "Hop in the RV! Eighth stop, Arizona," Papa says.

It took our Papa and us 12 hours to get here, but we finally made it. "People consider the Grand Canyon to be one of the seven wonders of the world. It is about 6,000 feet deep. Let's go water rafting!" momma says. "Hop in the RV!" Ninth stop, New Orleans," Papa says.

It took our Papa and us 22 hours to get here, but we finally made it. Our Papa likes to dance to jazz music. He moved his body, he moved his feet, and we danced all night on Bourbon Street. "Hop in the RV!" Tenth stop, Jackson, Mississippi," Papa says.

It took our Papa and us 3 hours to get here, but we finally made it. "We have to go to my alma mater," momma said. "Hey, Hey, look at the BOOM!" Step! Step! Go BOOM!" The halftime show is always the best when we come to these games!" Papa yelled. "Hop in the RV!" Eleventh stop, Miami," Papa says.

GO BOOM!

It took our Papa and us 13 hours to get here, but we finally made it. Gators were everywhere. "That's why they call Florida the SWAMP! South Beach is a few miles from here, let's head there to build sandcastles and pick up seashells. "Hop in the RV! Twelfth stop, Myrtle Beach!" Papa says.

It took our Papa and us 10 hours to get here, but we finally made it. "One of the most beautiful beaches in the world is Myrtle Beach." Mom said. "Can we swim with the dolphin's Papa?" Crystal asks. "YEAH!" Dennis and Tony exclaimed. "Hop in the RV!" Thirteenth stop, New York City," Papa says.

It took our Papa and us 10 hours to get here, but we finally made it. New York City, better known as "The Big Apple"! We must go visit the statue of Liberty. It represents freedom, liberty, and the United States itself. When we are finished here, we are going to scroll on over to Times Square! There is so much to see." Papa preached. "Hop in the RV!" Fourteenth stop, Philadelphia," Papa says.

It took our Papa and us 2 hours to get here, but we finally made it. We hopped off the RV and stood in front of a Food truck. "Street food from the city of brotherly love!" Dennis yelled. There were food trucks lined up for almost a mile. I want a Philly cheese steak with mushrooms, peppers, and onions y'all!" "Hop in the RV!" Fifteenth stop, Washington D.C.," Papa says.

It took our Papa and us 15 hours to get here, but we finally made it. "It looks even bigger in person!" Papa said. The White House is where the President and First Lady live. Washington D.C. is the nation's Capital. There is a lot of history here. "Let's not waste any more time, there is so much to see," Momma said. "Hop in the RV!" Sixteenth stop, Memphis," Papa says.

It took our Papa and us 13 hours to get here, but we finally made it. "It's nothing like music known as the BLUES. Give me my wig so I can act like Elvis! Papa danced on top of his RV! "Seventeenth stop, Nashville, Tennessee," Papa says.

It took our Papa and us 3 hours to get here, but we finally made it. There was a concert with country music playing. The family danced until we had sore feet and couldn't dance anymore to the beat. "Hop in the RV!" Eighteenth stop, Morehead, Kentucky," Papa says

It took our Papa and us 4 hours to get here, but we finally made it. "Look at the football player with number 19 on his jersey. He jumped into mid-air to catch that football with one hand! Go Eagles!" TOUCHDOWN!" They cheered. "Hop in the RV!" Nineteenth stop, Louisville, Kentucky," Papa says.

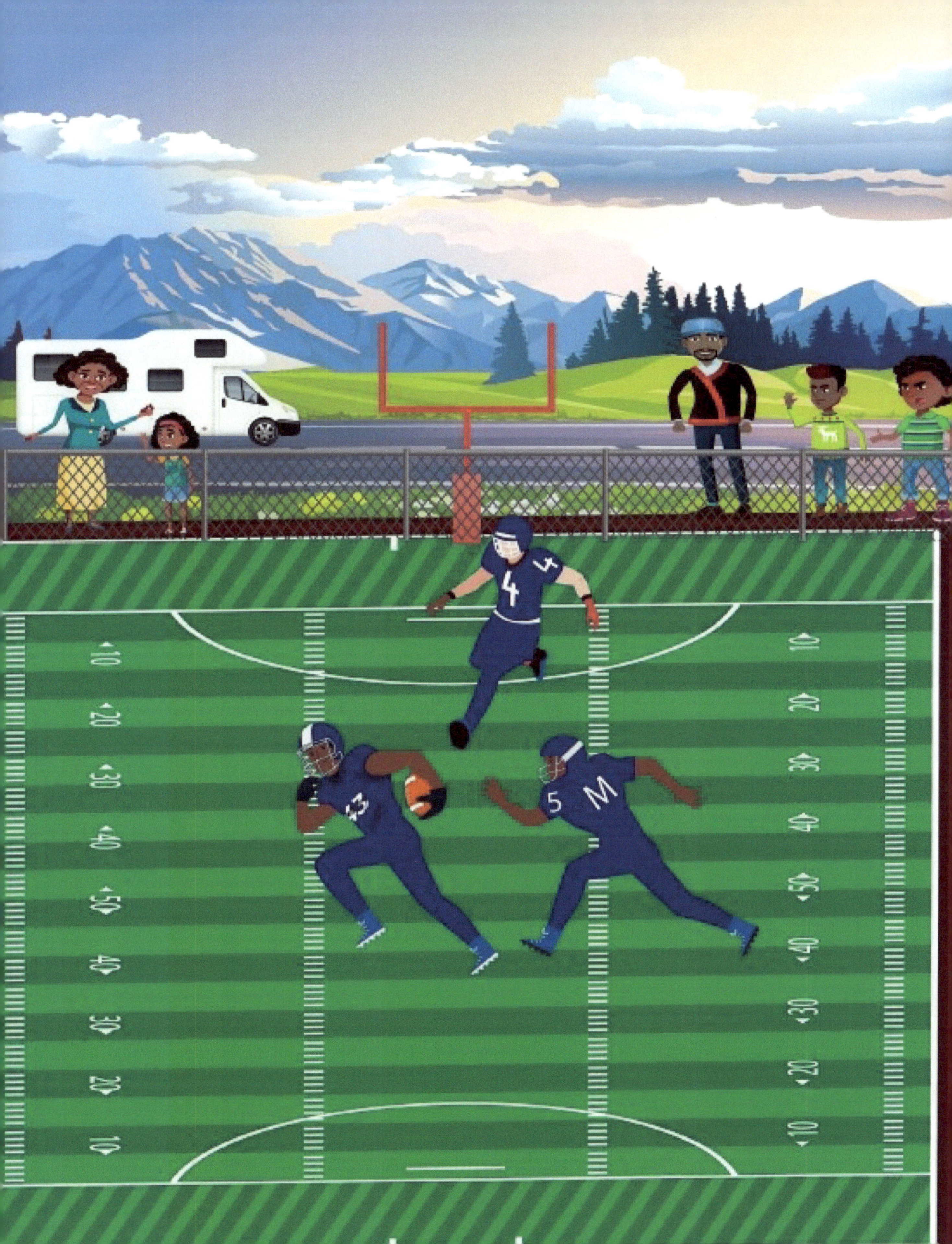

It took our Papa and us 2 hours to get here, but we finally made it. "Let's go see some horse racing!" Papa says. "We are back at our home, Home of The Kentucky Derby. We can tailgate at Churchill Downs." Dennis said. "This is my kind of place guys!" Tony shouts. We lit up the grill and threw steaks, burgers, and hot dogs on it. "AND THEY'RE OFF!" Yelled the announcer. What gorgeous thoroughbreds, Papa thought to himself. We are in our city, and there is no place like home.

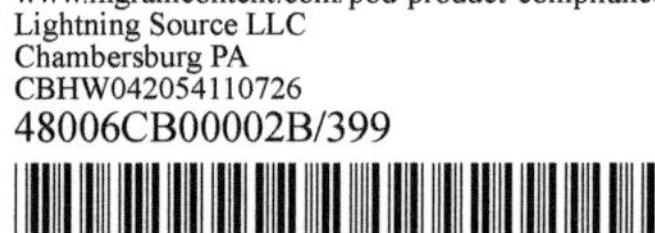

www.ingramcontent.com/pod-product-compliance
Lightning Source LLC
Chambersburg PA
CBHW042054110726
48006CB00002B/399